TODD TAYLOR'S
GOSPEL BANJO

FOREWORD BY FRED GRETSCH

To access audio visit:
www.halleonard.com/mylibrary

Enter Code
2328-6393-2447-8738

ISBN 978-1-57424-336-9
SAN 683-8022

Cover by James Creative Group

Al songs public domain. Arrangements by Todd Taylor. Recorded, mixed and engineered by Todd Taylor at Pirate Records.

Thanks.

The Gretsch Family

Fred & Dinah Gretsch

Joe Carducci

Joe Bonsall—The Oak Ridge Boys

GHS Strings Dave Cowles & Chris Walters

Mike Moody & Malinda Moody

David Cunningham, DC Banjo Works, Banjo Bridges

Peter Hoffman Banjo & Guitar Straps

Justin Reed "The Justin Reed Show", 88.3 FM, Murfreesboro, TN

Todd Taylor plays Gretsch Banjo's & Guitars and GHS Banjo Strings

Joey Sanchez caboots.com

Photographer - Ken Marler

Notation – Paul Hinton

Contents

Foreword

Pastor Marvin Sapp, one of today's best
contemporary gospel artists said, "Gospel
music allows us to become closer to God and
closer to each other." I know that's what Todd
Taylor wants to accomplish with this special
Gospel Banjo Book.

Todd has been blessed with a unique God-
given talent. He is an high-energy, creative
force and regarded as one of today's most
influential banjo artists. Like other music
pioneers, Todd is always moving forward. He
loves pushing boundaries with the banjo to go
beyond bluegrass, and has mastered a wide
range of music genres from Bach to Rock

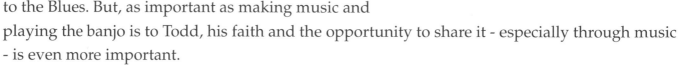

to the Blues. But, as important as making music and
playing the banjo is to Todd, his faith and the opportunity to share it - especially through music
- is even more important.

I am proud to call Todd a friend and have him as the official "face and fingers" of Gretsch
banjos. We couldn't have a finer endorser. The Gretsch family appreciates his passion and for
helping fuel the continuation of "That Great Gretsch Sound" which was started by my great-
grandfather in 1883.

I know you will enjoy this book. One of the best ways to enrich your life is by participating in
music!

Fred Gretsch

Word from the Author

I am happy to share my personal banjo arrangements of these well-known Gospel songs with you. The tablature arrangements follow each song on the accompanying online audio. I hope you enjoy playing along with me as you learn these favorite Gospel tunes.

www.toddtaylorbanjoman.com

Amazing Grace

Traditional - Arrangement by Todd Taylor

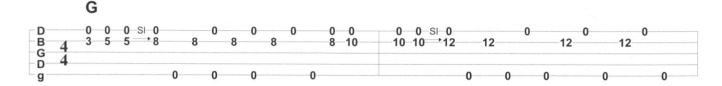

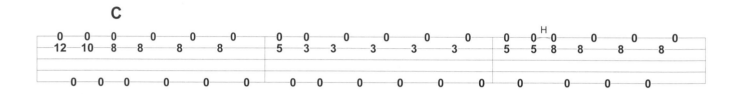

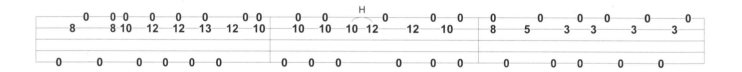

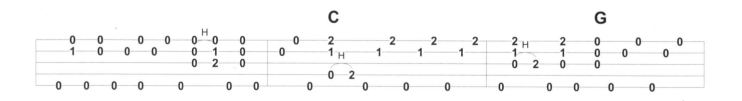

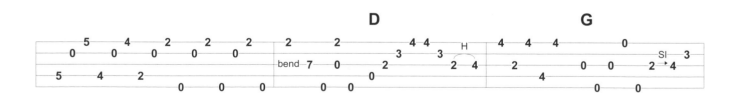

Page 1 / 3

6

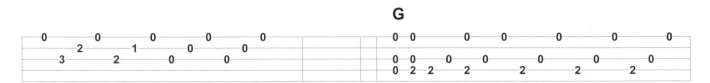

G

Dobro and fiddle breaks

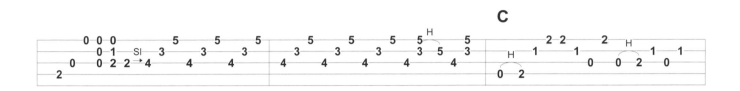

C

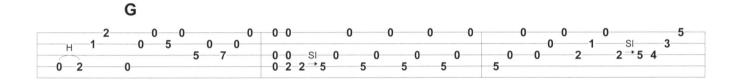

G

D

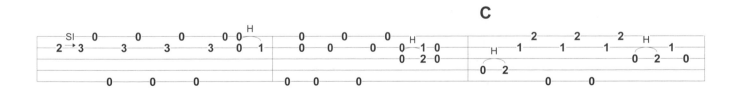

C

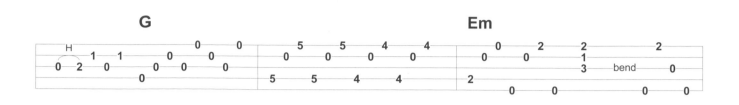

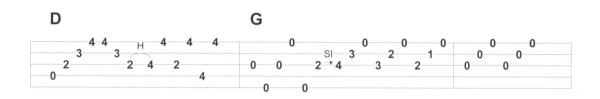

Todd Taylor & Mike Moody playing in Brooklyn New York street sounds.

How Great Thou Art

Key of C

Traditional - Arrangement by Todd Taylor

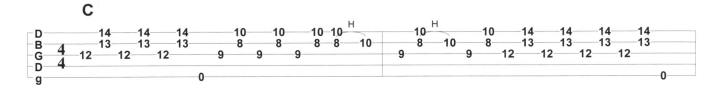

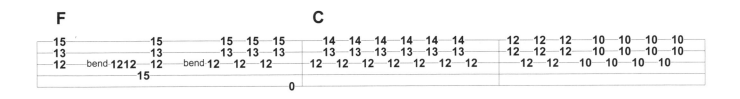

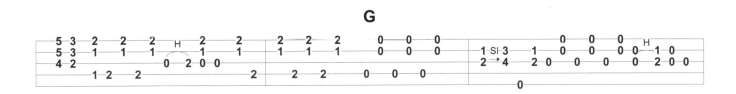

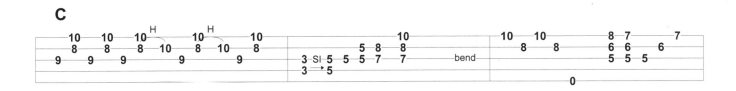

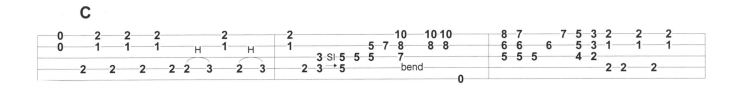

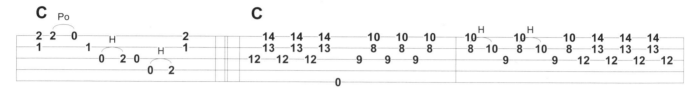

Dobro and fiddle breaks

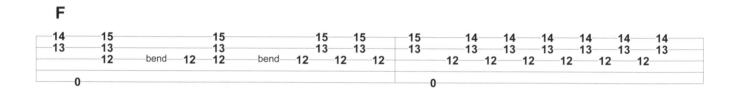

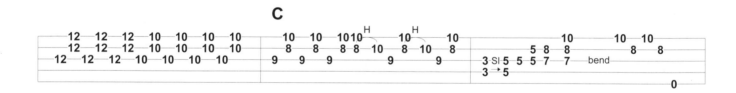

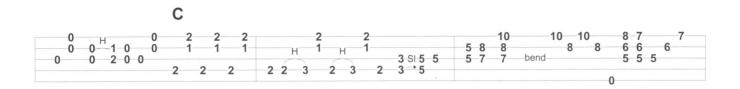

```
            C
0         0     2   2   2           2         2                          10        10  10      8  7        7
0   0 H 1 0 0   1   1   1     H 1   H 1                     5   8   8       8     8       6  6      6
0       0 2 0 0                             3 SI 5  5       5   7   7   bend              5   5  5
            2       2   2       2 2 3 2 3 2 3→5                                       0
```

```
      C                                                                 G             B
5 3   2   2   2 1     2     2   2   2   2   2              3   3   3     3   3   3
5 3   1   1   1 1 H   1     1   1   1   1   1              3   3   3     3   3   3
4 2             0   2 0 0                                  2   2   2   3   3   3
      2   2   2             2   2   2   2   2
```

```
G           C  Po                       H
5   5 5 7 5   2 2   0              2 9 10          10      10            10
3   3 5 6 5 0 1     1 0   2 0   H  1 8 8        8       8            8
4 4                            0 2  7 7   bend 7       7            7
```

Todd Taylor's world fastest banjo player ring.

Page 3 / 3

The Uncloudy Day

Key of G

Traditional - Arrangement by Todd Taylor

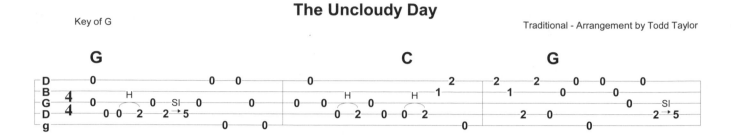

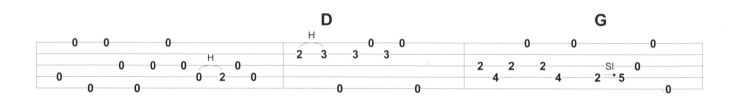

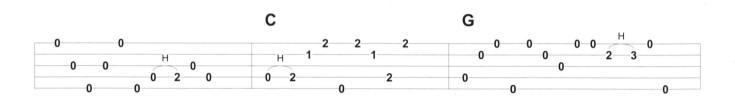

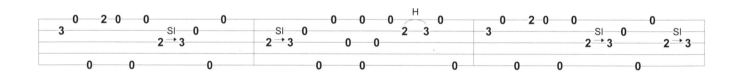

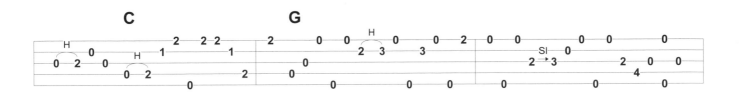

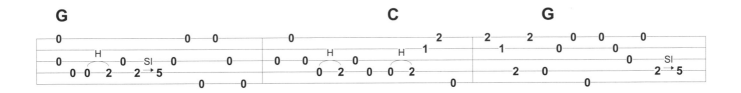

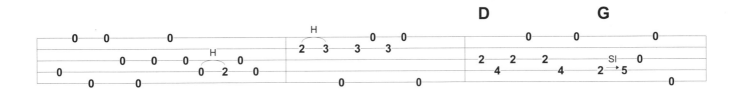

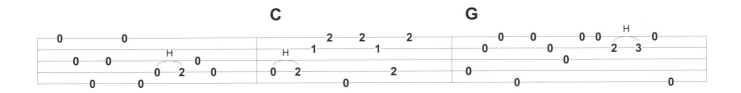

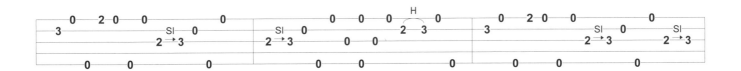

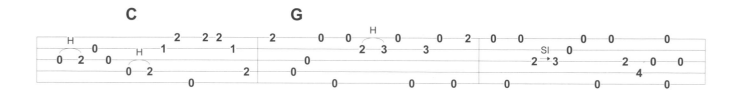

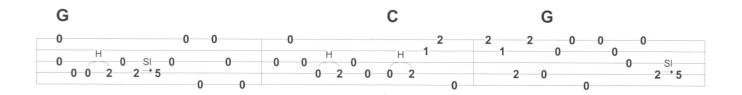

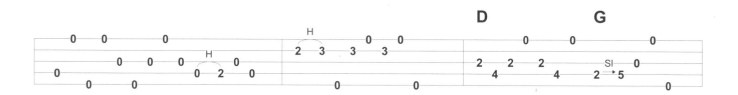

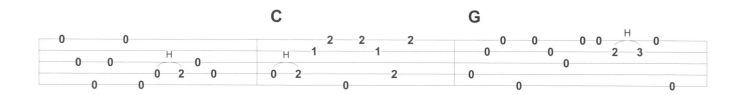

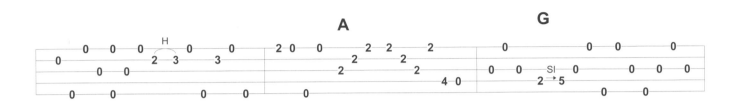

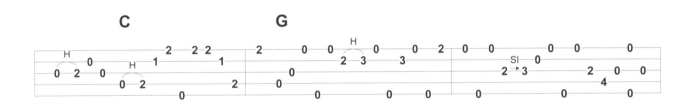

Todd Taylor with friends Jesse Cahill and Keith Picot of Cousin Harley in Chicago after show.

What a Friend We Have In Jesus

Key of G

Traditional - Arrangement by Todd Taylor

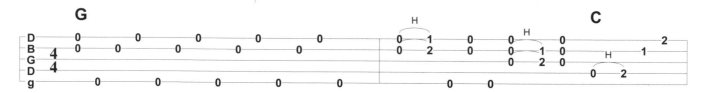

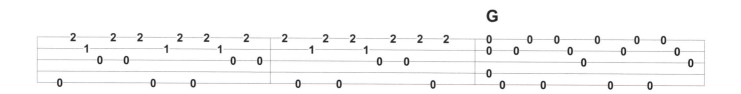

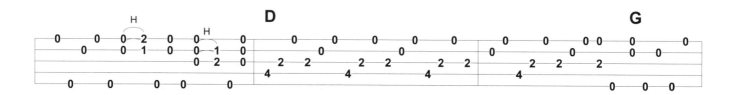

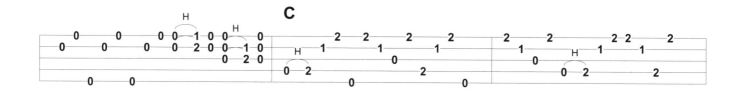

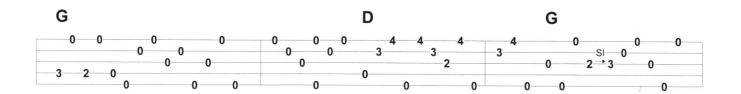

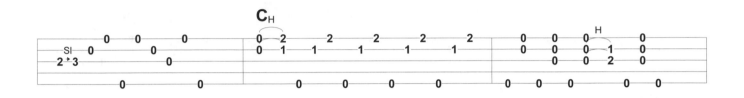

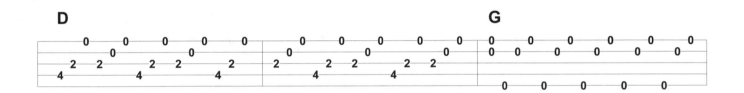

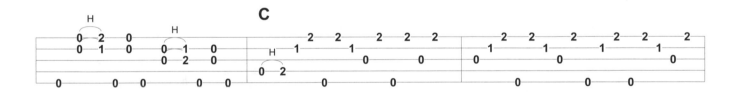

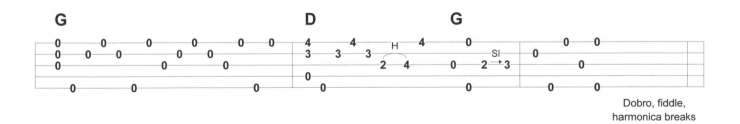

Dobro, fiddle,
harmonica breaks

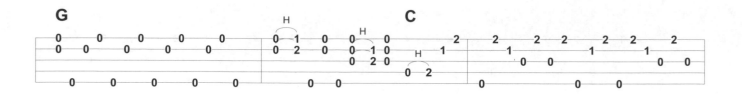

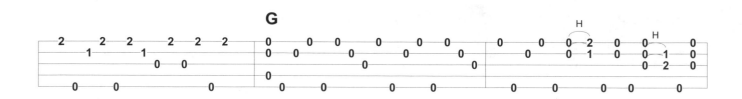

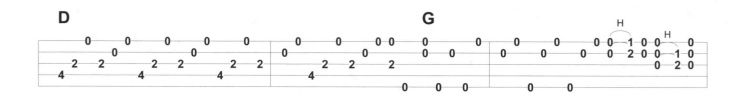

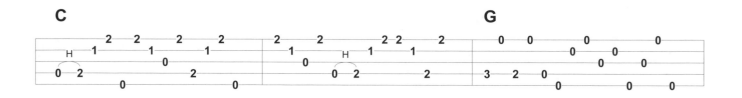

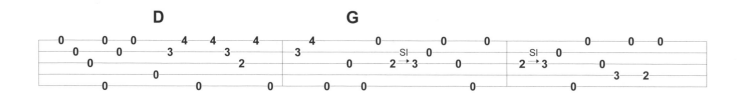

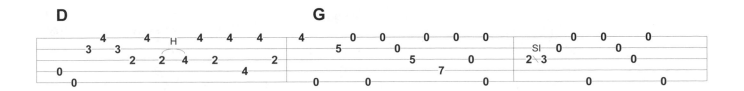

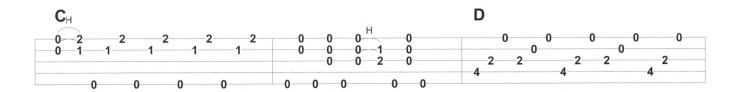

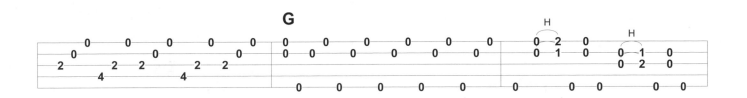

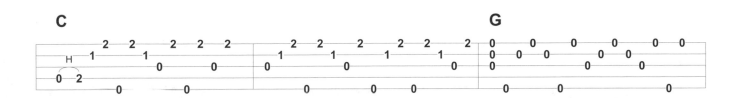

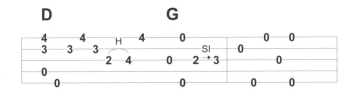

I'll Fly Away

Key of G

Traditional - Arrangement by Todd Taylor

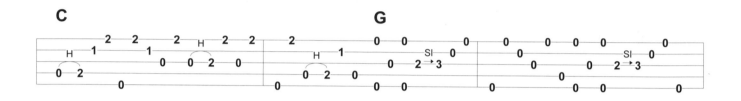

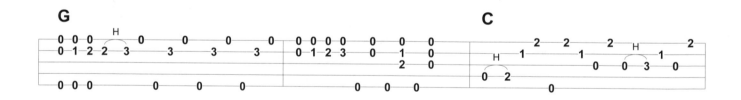

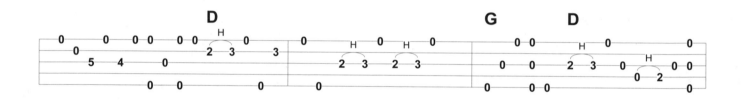

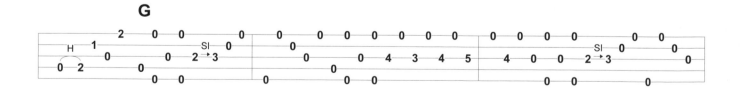

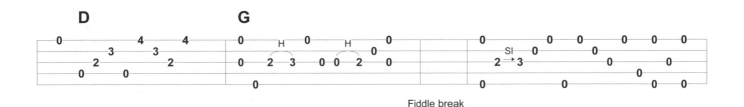

Fiddle break

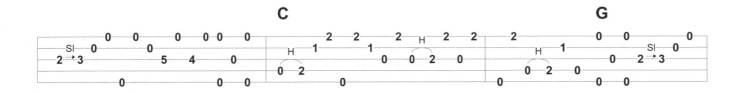

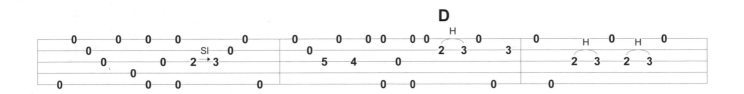

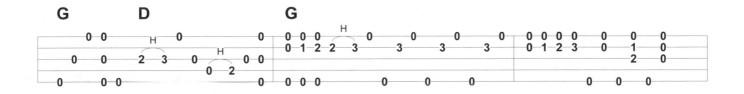

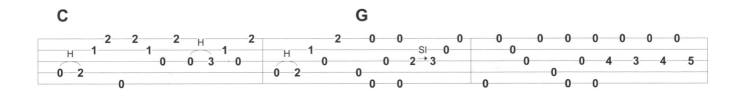

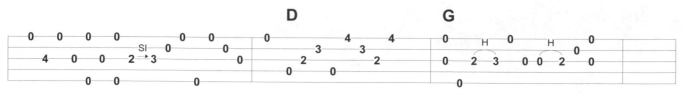

Dobro break

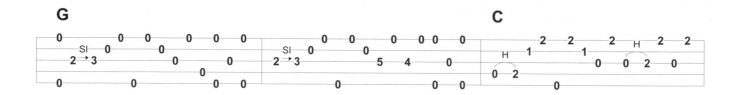

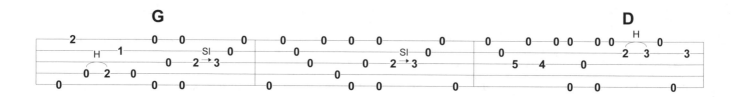

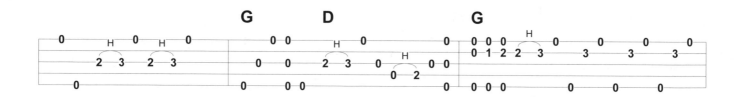

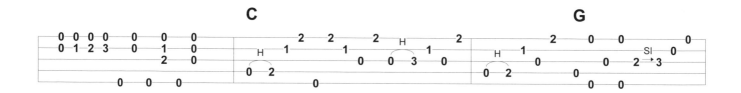

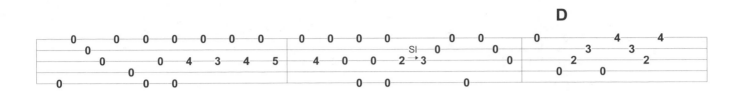

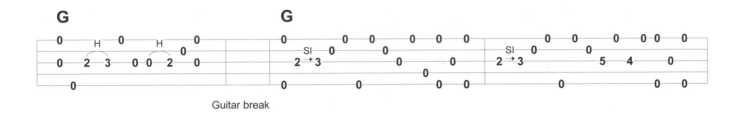

Guitar break

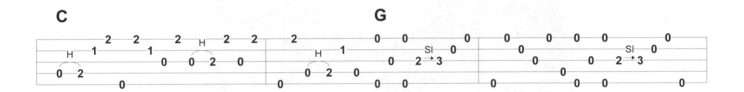

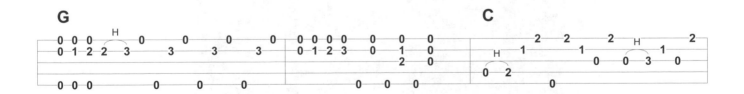

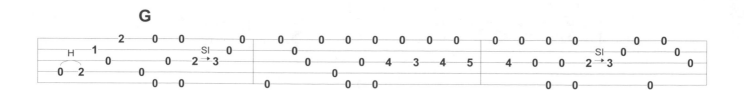

Todd Taylor.

Patriotic Medley

Key of C

Traditional - Arrangement by Todd Taylor

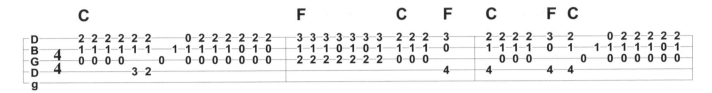

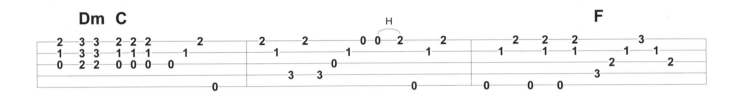

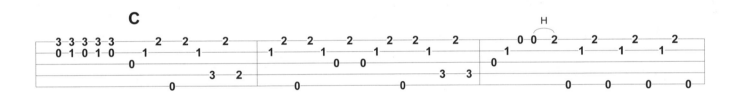

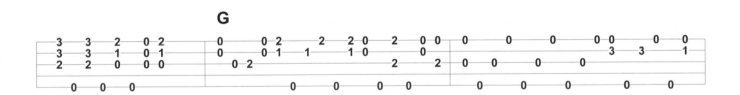

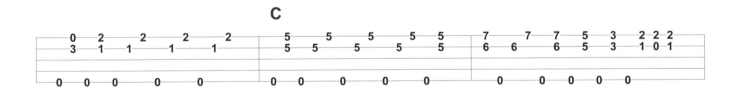

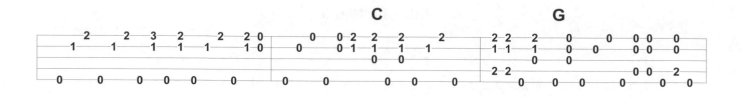

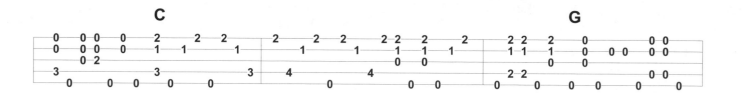

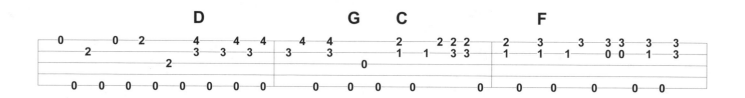

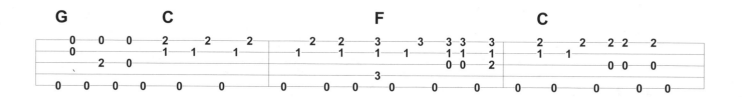

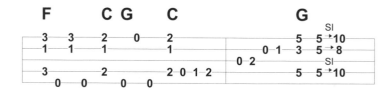

Wayfaring Stranger

Key of Em

Traditional - Arrangement by Todd Taylor

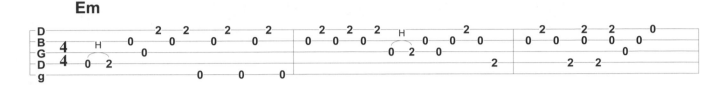

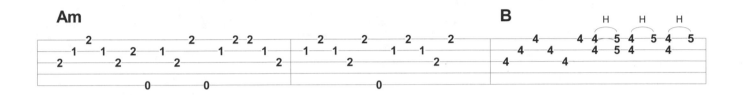

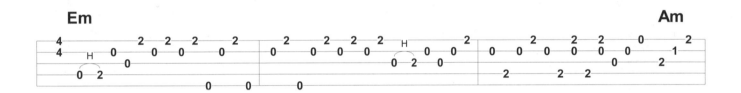

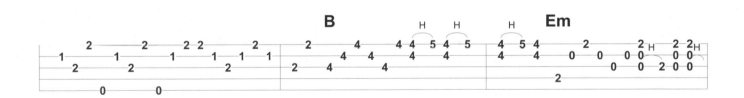

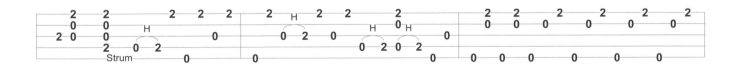

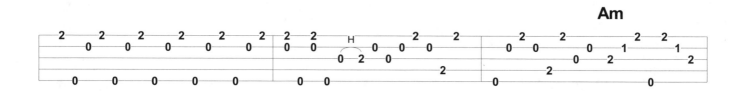

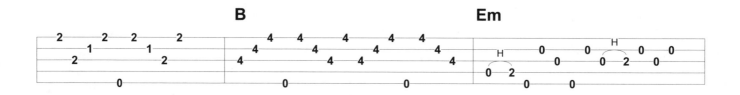

C

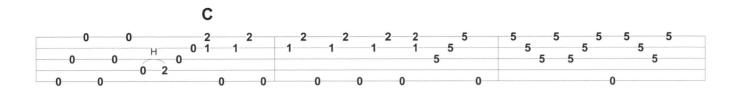

B   Em

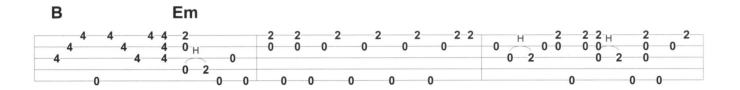

Am   B

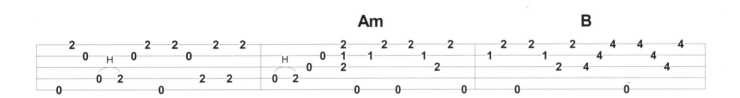

Em   Em

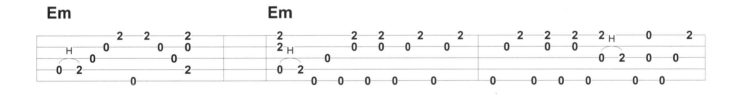

Fiddle break

Am   Em

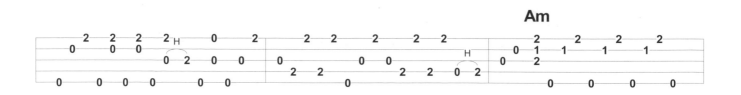

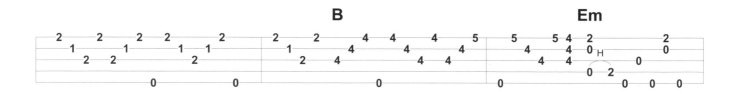

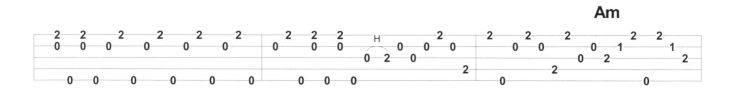

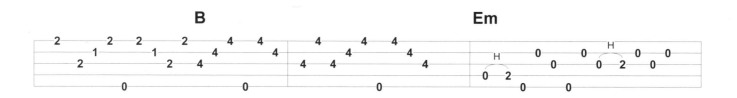

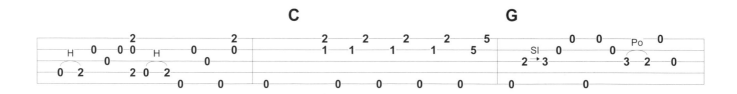

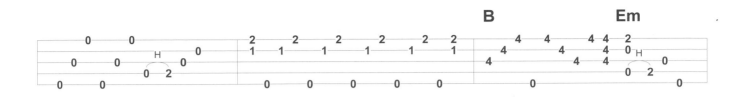

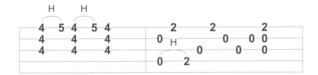

Todd Taylor and John Gatto, Guitarist for the Original
Band "The Good Rats" at Street Sounds, Brooklyn
New York playing White Falcons.

When the Roll Is Called Up Yonder

G Tuning

Traditional - Arrangement by Todd Taylor

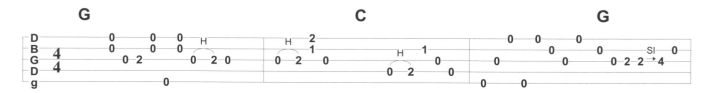

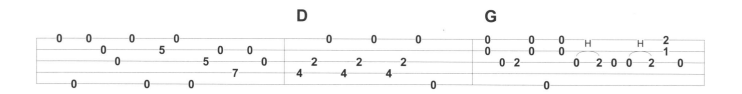

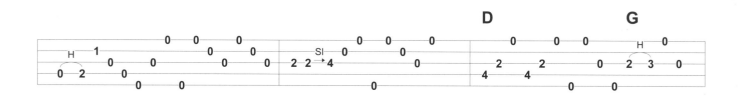

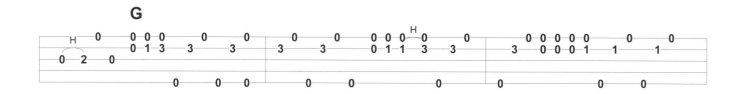

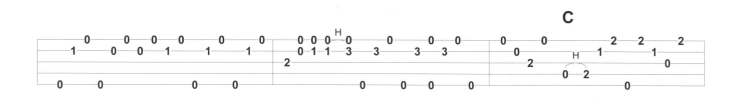

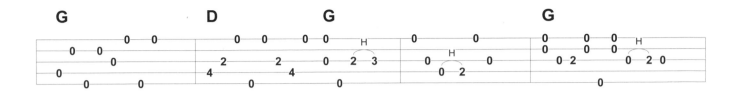

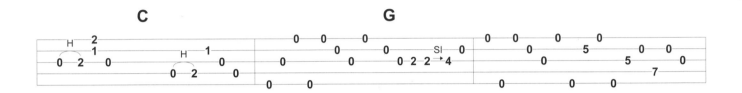

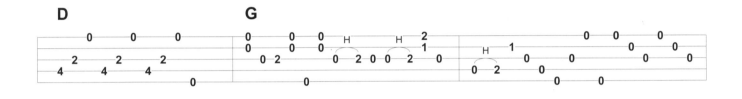

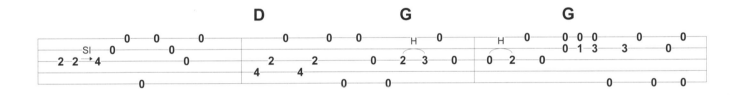

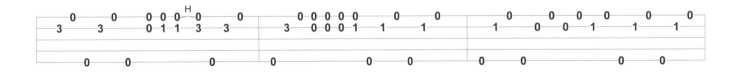

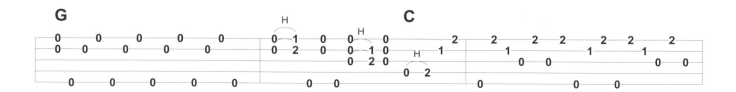

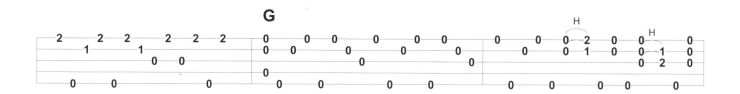

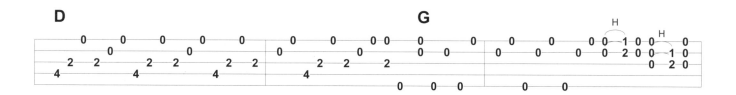

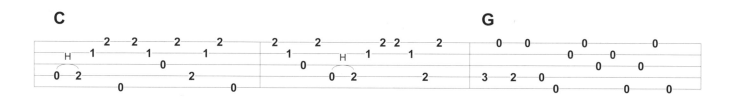

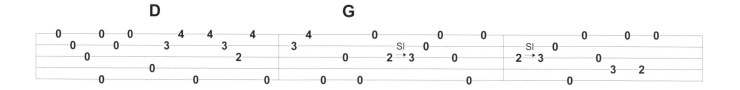

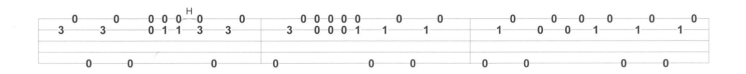

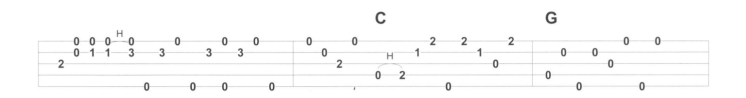

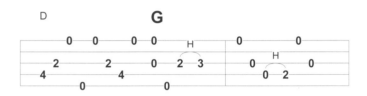

At the Country Music Hall of Fame, Todd Taylor, Fred Gretsch, Steve Wariner and Joe Carducci .

Page 4 / 4

Little Bessie

Capo at 4th fret

Traditional - Arrangement by Todd Taylor

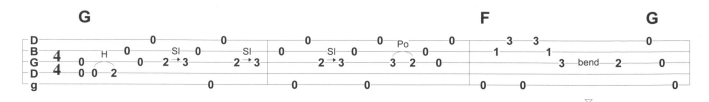

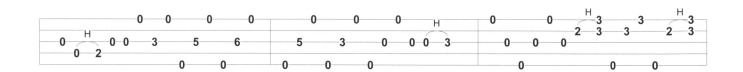

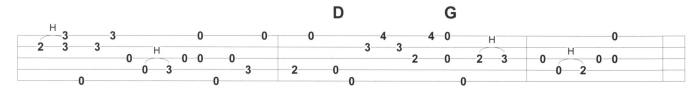

Vocals and mandolin breaks

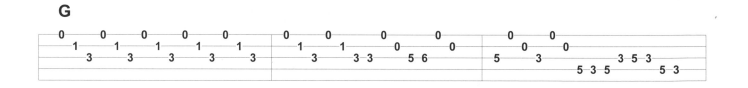

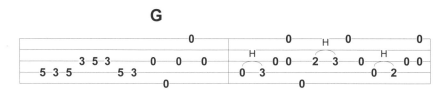

Guitar and vocals end the song

The Old Rugged Cross

Key of G

Traditional - Arrangement by Todd Taylor

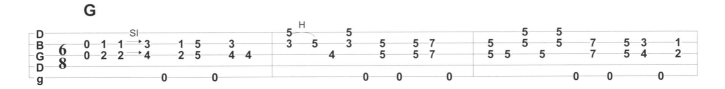

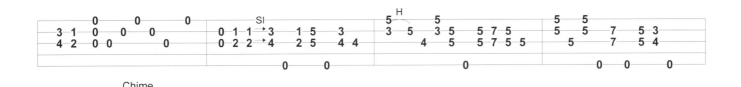

Chime

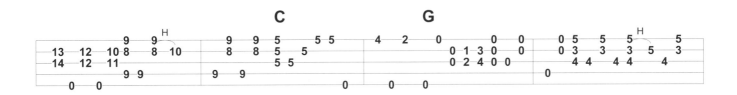

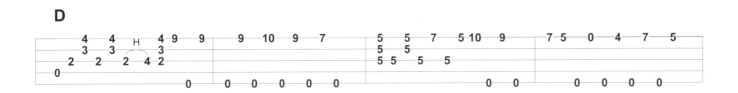

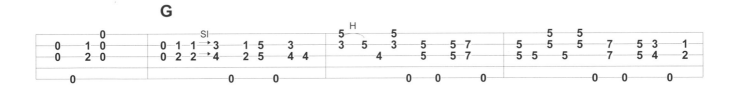

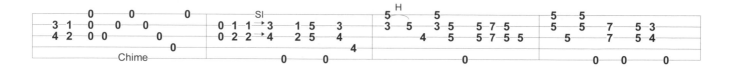

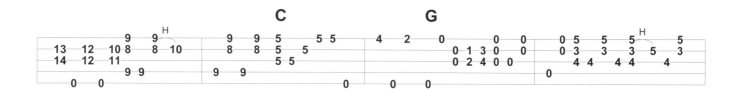

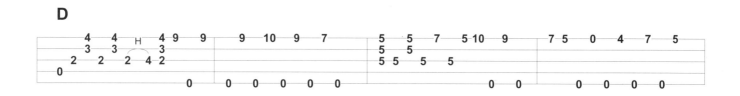

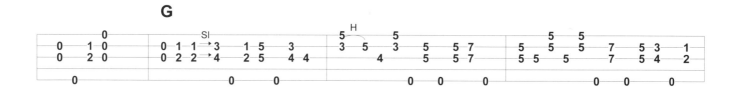

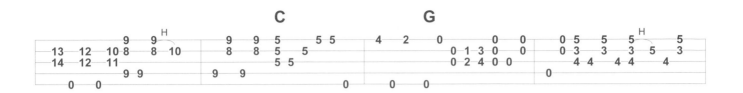

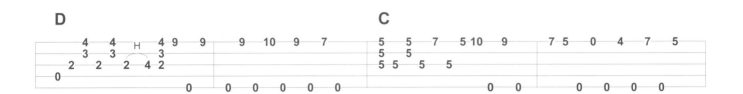

Todd Taylor.

About the Author

Todd "Banjoman" Taylor first fell in love with the banjo at just six years old. While on a family trip to Walt Disney World, Todd's parents realized he had wandered off. After a frantic search they found Todd on a steamboat ride -- mesmerized by the music of the banjo performer. His mom finally gave in to his pleadings and purchased his first banjo from a JC Penny catalog the following Christmas. Since then, Todd has enjoyed a music career spanning three decades.

As a teenager and young adult, he and his twin brother performed on the Grand Ole Opry with music legends Roy Acuff and Bill Monroe, and TV shows like Regis and Kathy Lee. Todd may be best known for using his unique style to elevate the banjo from the confines of bluegrass to build a bridge into all genres of music, especially rock 'n' roll. He was the first solo banjo musician featured on the Rick Dees Weekly Top 40 internationally-syndicated radio program in the 1980's for his groundbreaking arrangement and performance of Lynyrd Skynyrd's "Freebird."

Although Todd has donated his time to various worthwhile charities during his career, the Muscular Dystrophy Association (MDA) has a special place in his heart. In his twenties Todd became increasingly ill and almost lost his life. Extensive testing revealed he had inherited a mitochondrial disease, and despite his doctor's prognosis, Todd was determined to recover. He performed on the MDA telethon with Jerry Lewis on more than one occasion; increasing awareness of the disease and helping to raise funds for the organization's tireless efforts.

In 2007, Todd was the first to set the Guinness World Record for Fastest Banjo by performing both parts of "Dueling Banjos" at a mind-blowing 210 beats per minute! He dedicated his record to everyone fighting to overcome a disease or obstacle in their life, and continues to encourage others who may be struggling about the power of a positive attitude.

2011 produced Todd's rock 'n' blues tablature book, "Pickin' Over the Speed Limit", and a feature in the documentary Breaking and Entering, highlighting his Guinness World Record achievement. He has earned dozens of Grammy nominations over the past decade in multiple categories, from original song composition to producing. Todd's eighth and latest CD, *Indescribable*, earned six Grammy nominations -- most of them attributed to his performance of "Bach Cello Suite No. 1 in G Major," accompanied by Thornton Cline on cello and long-time friend Mike Moody on bass.

But the pinnacle of his career came in 2012 when Governor Nikki Haley presented Todd with the "Order of the Palmetto", the highest civilian honor in South Carolina, for his inspiring personal example and musical contribution to his home state. Todd says, "My life has been blessed in so many ways, and I have no plans to stop sharing the gift God has given me."

More Great Banjo Books from Todd Taylor...

More Great Banjo Books from Centerstream...

Those using
Centerstream
Books & DVDs

The Competition